Stacy Hutchison~
From the heart,
Craig

Lessons Learned While Cooking...

FROM THE HEART

Lessons Learned While Cooking...

FROM THE HEART

A heartfelt sharing of personal stories
and great Cajun comfort-food recipes.
Together, they will touch your heart,
warm your soul, and fill your belly.

Craig J. McKneely

Always Productions
San Diego, California

The following trademarks appear throughout this book: Campbell's Condensed Cream of Chicken Soup; Campbell's Condensed Cream of Mushroom Soup; Coke; Dr. Pepper; Duncan Hines Moist Deluxe German Chocolate Cake Mix; Duncan Hines Moist Deluxe White Cake Mix; Eagle Brand Condensed Milk; Hormel Boneless Smoked Pork Chops; Jell-O; Knorr Concentrated Chicken Flavor Broth; Kraft Grated Parmesan Cheese; Louisiana Seasoned Fish Fry; Magnalite; Oak Grove Smokehouse Creole Jambalaya Mix; Philadelphia Cream Cheese; Pillsbury Grands! Buttermilk Biscuits; Sprite; Tabasco Sauce; Tony Chachere's Original Seasoning; Velveeta Cheese; Zatarain's Gumbo Filé; Zatarain's Seasoned Fish Fry.

First printing 2002

ISBN 0-9719367-4-9
LCCN 2002091118

ATTENTION CORPORATIONS, UNIVERSITIES, COLLEGES, AND PROFESSIONAL ORGANIZATIONS: Quantity discounts are available on bulk purchases of this book for educational, gift purposes, or as premiums for increasing magazine subscriptions or renewals. Special books or book excerpts can also be created to fit specific needs. For information, please contact Always Productions, P.O. Box 33836, San Diego, CA 92163-3836.

To Love

A portion of the proceeds from this book
will be donated to children's charities.

Acknowledgments

I would first like to thank God for this incredible adventure. Without God in my heart, and by my side, I would have given up a long time ago. Grandma McKneely, thank you for your belief in me…always. Mama, thank you for your endless love and humor. Daddy, thank you for still being with me even today.

To anyone who has shared a meal at my table, I thank you. It was your praise that gave me the courage to pursue this dream. Wow! Dreams really do come true.

I'd also like to thank my family of friends: Debbie Bresler, Mark Boveri, Mary Lanier, Anne Decareaux, Hope Schneider, Grammy, Jim Lestelle, Gary Heflin, Faye Williams, Stephanie Yang, Sandi McDonald, Dion Mial, Todd Kuebler, Curt Lewis, Ian Bode, Mike Simons, Michael Magee, Michael Edwards, Michael Junot, Jimmy Lacour, Craig Wilgenbusch, Bobby Edelson, Andrew Brooks, Rob Trujillo, and Dale Bucek. I love you one and all!

Jodi, Janner, Makayla and Bruce, I love you dearly. You too Vernon! You are in my heart, thoughts and prayers each and every day.

To Patti LaBelle, thank you for being my hero. To Della Reese, thanks for being my role model.

I am the result of every person I've ever met; from the inner-city youth of Orleans Parish to famous Hollywood celebrities, from welfare moms to state and local politicians, from participants in my training classes to strangers on the street that shared a warm smile. I have gained much from each of you. Thank you.

Contents

Lessons Learned While Cooking . . .

Welcome to
My Heart and
My Kitchen

For the past 40 years, my heart has seen, done and felt more than most. Honestly, I would prefer you never experience what I've endured. This book is not just a testament to my life—the good, the bad and the ugly—but also to my unending faith. "What doesn't kill us makes us stronger." Since I'm still breathing, I must be pretty damn strong. For that, I am forever grateful. If I can share some of that strength and love with you, then my mission here will be complete.

I also hope to inspire and comfort those that may have had similar experiences. Know that you're not alone; physically or spiritually. Not one of us on earth has walked a path that doesn't already have footprints on it from someone else. Also know those

1

loved ones that have gone on before us are watching and surrounding us with their unconditional love. Take comfort in their presence and talk to them...just as you did before. I firmly believe they are listening.

For me, cooking is an expression of love; my love. It's personal. To cook for total strangers is very awkward for me. That's why I've not pursued a career as a chef or in catering. When you sit at my table, your belly is filled and your heart knows it. The few times I've messed up a meal have been when my heart just wasn't there. I've since learned that lesson...the hard way!

As you read the recipes and prepare the dishes, know that your heart needs to be there as well. Let the food on your table be an expression of your love, not just another dinner. There is a difference and I challenge you to experience it. You can do it, I promise.

Think about some of the meals you've experienced in the past. Grandma's are usually known for being the best cooks. Why? Because of the love they pour into every dish. Other meals may have been good, but something was missing. It was love. You can taste the difference.

There are a few things you will quickly notice about the recipes in my book. First of all, I'm not shy about sharing my favorite brands and products. I've tried many and these are my favorites. The manufacturers haven't paid me a dime to use their products or to write about them. Because I care more about you having the best results possible than I do about who's paying, I share honestly. I invite you to trust me and take advantage of my many years of trial-and-error in the kitchen.

Second, you will notice an absence of certain ingredients; namely garlic and bell pepper. Most Cajun recipes are filled with the stuff. The reason I don't cook with a lot of either is because they make me burp; plain and simple. Since Cajun cooking is much more about cooking from the heart than following a recipe word-for-word, if you like garlic, add garlic. If you like bell pepper, go for it. If you want it more or less spicy, you have the power to change it. The hardest part of writing this book has been converting the feelings of the heart into measured ingredients. Baby, cook from <u>your</u> own heart.

Each recipe has a section titled "Psst..." This section has tips, suggestions, and variations to help make your dish a success. I firmly believe nobody is smart enough to make a mistake that hasn't already been made. Again, take advantage of my mistakes and experience.

So share your heart as you cook. Remember to do what feels right to you and don't be afraid to experiment. Try new things and change the old things *a bit. Fill the bellies and warm the hearts of those you love. They will love and remember you for it, I promise!*

Baby, fat people get hungry and I gotta eat! Let's get this party started...

*"When you lock others out
of your heart, you lock yourself in.
While it may be safe,
it's also very lonely."*

*"Love yourself, Baby . . .
warts and all."*

First, You Start with a Roux...

Since most Cajun recipes begin with a roux, it's only fitting the book start there, too.

I can still hear my Grandma McKneely singing "Amazing Grace" in the kitchen while cooking. She knew every verse, and those she didn't, she made up. What she didn't know then was she was teaching me about cooking...from the heart. Love was in every bite of food she prepared. She was a beautiful lady and a wonderful cook. With a song like "Amazing Grace" on her lips, how could she go wrong?

Just as a roux is often the foundation of Cajun cooking, so is the heart the foundation of _my_ cooking. Cooking is an expression of who I am, what I am, and where I began. It's my way of going through your belly to touch your heart. It's another way of me saying "I love you."

One of the "side effects" of cooking from the heart is the wonderful aromas created in the kitchen. When you walk into my home, it <u>smells</u> like home. There is nothing like the smell of a pork roast cooking in the oven or a gumbo on the stove simmering for hours. Even something as simple as a roux will fill the home with a sense of comfort that envelops all that enter.

I invite you to open your heart as you read each story and recipe. Allow yourself to remember, to feel, and to love. Don't be afraid if it stirs up some old memories. Your heart will thank you for it as well as those that sit at your table. This book is all about holding on to your faith, healing your heart, loving yourself, and sharing that love with others.

And so it is...you start with a roux.

Roux

1 cup vegetable oil
1½ cups all-purpose flour

In a heavy skillet, heat oil on medium heat. Add flour and stir continuously. Once the flour starts to brown, lower heat to medium-low. Continue stirring non-stop until roux is deep brown; usually 35–45 minutes or even an hour.

Psst...

Cast iron and Magnalite skillets are my favorites. Baby, don't try to make a roux in a flimsy lightweight skillet or one that's got a non-stick surface. "That dog don't hunt!"

Only use all-purpose flour for roux. Don't use self-rising flour.

There are two secrets to a great roux. 1) Stir constantly. I prefer to use a metal spatula instead of a spoon to stir roux. The spoon doesn't have the flat surface to keep the roux moving like a spatula does. 2) Don't let the fire get too hot. If you try to cook a roux too fast, it will burn. If you burn the roux, you may as well throw it out and start over because your food will taste burnt too.

Caution—a cooking roux is hotter than hell. If you get carried away with the stirring and it splashes on your skin, you will know it. Be careful, Baby.

The roux is done when it's dark like melted chocolate.

Roux can be stored in the refrigerator for up to a few weeks. Add just a few tablespoons to darken, thicken and flavor gravies.

"Cut the drama and just live your life."

Learning to Cook

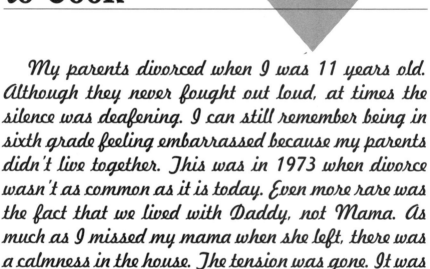

My parents divorced when I was 11 years old. Although they never fought out loud, at times the silence was deafening. I can still remember being in sixth grade feeling embarrassed because my parents didn't live together. This was in 1973 when divorce wasn't as common as it is today. Even more rare was the fact that we lived with Daddy, not Mama. As much as I missed my mama when she left, there was a calmness in the house. The tension was gone. It was sad and yet peaceful at the same time.

My fascination with cooking was partly born out of necessity. Daddy was a horrible cook and was the first to admit it. He could hold his own on a backyard grill, but Baby, the kitchen was completely foreign to him.

I don't know what made this 11-year-old child think, in the absence of his mother, _he_ was responsible for taking over her role. Maybe it was because I was the oldest child. Maybe because Daddy was such a bad cook. Maybe because this scared little boy was seeking the love and approval of adults. Whatever the reason, my cooking "from the heart" lessons were just starting.

After Mama left, I found an old red cookbook tucked in a kitchen cabinet. In a matter of no time, I was baking cakes from scratch. Success, and the desired approval from adults, pushed me forward.

To this day, I still have an incredible "maternal energy" about me. Not quite the norm for a grown man, but then who wants to be that normal? Sure, I may have been robbed of my childhood, but look at me now. Some people are so vanilla they have no flavor at all. I'm proud of my flavor; no matter what it took to get it!

Black-Eyed Peas

1 tablespoon margarine

1 large onion chopped

1 pound dried black-eyed peas

2 stalks celery chopped fine

4 bay leaves

1 bunch green onions

1 teaspoon dried tarragon

½ cup chopped fresh parsley

1 pound smoked sausage cut into bite-size pieces

2 tablespoons Knorr Concentrated Chicken Flavor Broth

Tony Chachere's Original Seasoning

Sort through dried peas to remove any "bad" ones. Soak four–six hours in a large bowl of water.

In a stockpot, sauté onions and celery in margarine until transparent. Add sausage. Continue to sauté until sausage begins to brown. Pour off any remaining water from the soaking peas. Add peas to the pot with enough water to cover the peas plus about two inches. Add Knorr chicken flavor broth, tarragon, parsley and green onions. Stir well. Bring to a boil. Lightly season with Tony Chachere's. Continue to cook at a rolling boil until peas are breaking apart and the gravy is thickened; about 1½ hours uncovered. (Add a little water if needed.) Season to taste with Tony Chachere's. Serve over white rice.

Psst...

I love to use a pound of smoked sausage and three smoked ham hocks. You can use whatever meat you like; ham, turkey sausage, or even a ham bone.

Baby, there ain't nothing better than sitting down to plate of black-eyed peas and rice with some hot Jiffy cornbread on the side. While others would be happy to make it a meal, I prefer to have some meat there too…fried chicken, pork chops, pork roast, etc.

"Baby, get off your rut and make it happen."

Divorce
and Children

When I was 13, my daddy remarried. As I put this on paper, I can hear Grandma McKneely say, "If you can't say anything nice, don't say anything at all." In honor of her spirit, let it suffice to say my daddy's new wife was my stepmonster. That's right, stepMonster! She was mentally, emotionally, and at times physically abusive. My siblings and I were the targets of her abuse. She would beat us while Daddy was at work and threaten us with another if we told him about it. The abuse from the stepbrothers was even worse. I remember feeling hopeless because I couldn't protect my siblings from this unending abuse. I cried a lot then and had little or no self-esteem.

To escape the madness and abuse, I always looked forward to spending a few weeks during the summer with Grandma and Grandpa McKneely in Jordoche, Louisiana. In this very small farm-town, the world seemed so much brighter. Even before the stepmonster,

Fordoche was always a sanctuary to me. My grandparents treated us like priceless treasures. It was safe. Their home was filled with pure unconditional love.

When I graduated from high school, I wrote my grandparents a letter; telling them about the abuse and begging them to let me move in with them. Of course they said, "Yes." Although I had to commute an hour each way to attend LSU (Louisiana State University), it was well worth it. I'd never felt so loved and protected in my entire life.

As a child, one of my favorite comfort foods was my grandma's french fries and eggs. During summer vacations, I would ask for it everyday for lunch. Grandma would ask, "Aren't you tired of that yet?" It's a very simple recipe, but brings back some wonderful, heartfelt memories. To you, Grandma!

French Fries and Eggs

1 large red potato

2 eggs

Splash of milk

Vegetable oil

Salt and pepper

Wash the potato and remove any bad spots, but do not peel. Slice into french fries. (The thinner the better.) In a large skillet, deep-fry the potatoes in vegetable oil until well done. When the potatoes are done, remove from oil and drain on paper towel. While the french fries are draining, pour oil from the skillet; leaving a thin coating in the bottom of the pan.

Scramble two eggs in a bowl. Add a splash of milk. Scramble again. Return french fries to the hot skillet. Pour the scrambled eggs over the french fries and cook on medium to medium-high heat until the eggs are done; stirring and flipping as necessary.

Season with salt and pepper. Serve with catsup on the side.

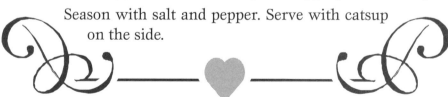

Psst...

This has to be one of the simplest recipes ever, but the taste is incredible. Give it a try!

Treat stepchildren as your own. Remember, you chose them. They didn't choose you. When they are grown and on their own, what will they have to say about you? How do you want to be remembered?

Daddy's Final Lesson

My dad was a bit of a workaholic. He loved his kids dearly, but was not always the best at showing it.

This changed when he was diagnosed with leukemia. During his two-year battle with that horrible disease, he taught all of us kids to "Stop and smell the roses, live life to its fullest and tell people when you love them."

My daddy died when he was 39. I was 19. His lesson has served me very well through the years. Whether it's family or friends, I end every phone call with "I love you." I have no problem saying those three precious words that everyone longs to hear.

Garth Brooks' song "If Tomorrow Never Comes" set Daddy's lesson to music. The movie "Ghost" brought it to the big screen. My heart brought it to everyday life.

Once when Daddy was in the hospital, in complete isolation, he had a craving for blackberry cobbler. All of his food had to be sterilized because of the risk of infection. He said it didn't matter what it tasted like, he just wanted some. My grandma said she would make the cobbler and bring it to him if I'd pick the berries. Deal!

When I got back to Fordoche, I went picking blackberries off the railroad track. It was a hot summer day and all that was between me and God was a pair of shorts and some flip-flops on my feet. I was almost done picking berries when I heard a rattling noise. Keeping in mind Daddy's lesson "stop and smell the roses," I thought about how cool it was to hear the dry grasses blowing in the wind. When I looked down between my feet, I saw the rattles of a rattlesnake. About six feet away was his head; ready to strike. Everything went into slow motion. I backed out, grabbed my blackberries and went home. I have never picked blackberries since. I love you, Daddy!

Fried Cabbage

**1 head green cabbage
(cored, cut in half, then each half into quarters)**
1 large onion chopped
½ pound bacon (cut in 1" strips)
Tony Chachere's Original Seasoning

In a large skillet, sauté bacon on medium heat until bacon is cooked and almost crispy. Stir often to prevent the skillet from burning. Add chopped onions and cook until onions are transparent. Pour off any excess bacon grease.

Add cabbage; breaking any large pieces into smaller ones with your hands. Stir well, bringing the onions and bacon to the top. Cook partially covered on medium heat until cabbage is tender. Do not overcook. Add Tony Chachere's to taste.

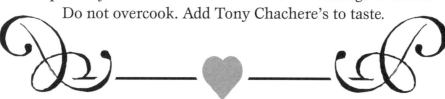

Psst...

To release the seasoning from the bottom of the skillet, you may want to add 2–3 tablespoons of water before you add the cabbage. Stir well to dissolve the flavor into the water.

I also like to add fresh cracked black pepper; just my personal taste. Leftovers are great the next day heated in the microwave.

Daddy loved cabbage. As a kid, I would not eat it at all. Grandma McKneely would stink up the whole house steaming cabbage. I love this recipe and not just for New Year's Day either.

"The nerve of some people's children."
—Grandma McKneely

The Darkest Day

My daddy's death was the darkest day of my life. I was 19 and scared as hell; trying to pretend to be stronger than I really felt.

His funeral fell on my shoulders. Daddy's divorce from my stepmonster became final just 30 days earlier. My grandparents were too distraught to help with the funeral arrangements. I'd already picked out the casket and made the preliminary arrangements months earlier. Picking out his clothes and bringing them to the funeral home was hard for me...very hard. Dealing with the financial aspects of his funeral almost pushed me right over the edge.

When the day was done and I was driving back to Fordoche, I remember the weather changing suddenly. The sun had been shining just two miles earlier and now it was raining cats and dogs, but not a cloud in the sky. The rain seemed to be blowing into the windshield. Seeing this, I remembered how much Daddy loved to get caught in the rain. (I hated it and he knew it!) I looked up through the windshield and said out loud, "Daddy, I guess you made it." I took it as a sign.

A few minutes passed and I reached for the velvet pouch containing his jewelry. I pulled out his watch and became furious because it was still ticking. "How dare you? My daddy is dead and you've got the nerve to keep ticking." It just didn't seem fair.

In that instant, I realized time goes on. Even without my daddy, time would keep moving forward. Pretty powerful stuff considering it was raining from my eyes as hard as it was outside the car.

The remainder of the drive was much different. I realized the rest of my life would be a piece of cake. Nothing could be any harder than burying my daddy at the age of 19. Even if others died, or if I had to face other crippling losses, I would be older, wiser and stronger.

You know, I was right.

Dirty Rice

1 tablespoon margarine	½ onion chopped
1–1½ pounds ground beef	½ cup fresh parsley chopped
6 ounces fresh mushrooms sliced	1 bunch green onions chopped
4 cups cooked white rice	Fresh cracked black pepper

½ pound smoked sausage diced into small pieces
Tony Chachere's Original Seasoning

In a large, heavy pot, sauté onion in margarine until it begins to brown. Add ground beef. Using a large cooking spoon, break apart the ground beef as it cooks. When the beef is done and beginning to brown, add the sausage, mushrooms, parsley and green onions. Continue to cook, stirring frequently until all ingredients are done and most of the liquid in the bottom of the pot has been reduced. Season to taste with Tony Chachere's and fresh cracked black pepper.

Add cooked white rice and stir until well blended. Remove from heat and serve hot.

Psst...

There are so many things you can add to this recipe; shrimp, celery, garlic, bell pepper, tasso, ground turkey or crawfish. Have fun with it and make it your own! It's your party.

This rice dressing is great as stuffing for the Thanksgiving turkey or everyday bell peppers.

You can even use leftover cooked white rice for this recipe.

"You either have fear or you have faith, but you can't have both."

Grandma McKneely

My dad's mom was my first friend. I can still remember as a small kid, when she and my grandpa came over to visit, my grandma would leave the company of the adults and come to my room. She and I would sit in the floor and color for what seemed like hours. And she could color good, too! She always stayed in the lines and sometimes outlined the picture in a different color before coloring the middle.

She always believed in me; no matter what I decided to do. She was always there. She believed in me long before I believed in myself. For her unconditional love, I am forever thankful.

At her funeral, I looked around the room and thought about how every person there was better off having known her. She was a beautiful person; inside and out. I expected to have been more emotional at her funeral, but realized there was nothing left undone.

She knew how much I loved her and I certainly knew how much she loved me. It was her time to go and I was thankful for the time I shared with her. She will always live on...in my heart. You see, love <u>never</u> dies.

As a kid, you know the age where all kids hate vegetables, my grandma played a trick on us that lasted many years. When she asked if we liked eggplant, the grandkids would all say, "No!" She would then ask if we liked fried fish. We always replied with a resounding, "Yes!" She served us fried eggplant and told us it was fried fish. We ate every bite and would ask Grandpa where he caught so many fish. It wasn't until years later that she admitted what she had done.

Every time I make fried eggplant, I smile as I think of her...soft wrinkled hands, saintly personality, heartwarming smile, gentle heart and all.

Thank you Grandma. I love you!

Grandma's Fried Eggplant

3 eggs   splash of milk

pinch of salt   Vegetable oil

1 eggplant—you know, the big purple kind

1 bag Louisiana Seasoned Fish Fry

Peel eggplant. Slice into very thin pieces about two inches wide by five inches long. (The thinner the better.) Soak in ice water with a pinch of salt added.

Heat oil in a heavy skillet. While waiting on the oil to heat, beat eggs in a large bowl. Add splash of milk. Place 4–5 pieces of eggplant in mixture. In a large plastic bowl with a lid or a large Ziploc bag, or even a paper bag, empty contents of Louisiana Seasoned Fish Fry. Lift each piece of eggplant individually, allowing the excess egg and milk to fall back in the bowl, then drop into the Fish Fry and shake. When the oil is hot, shake excess Fish Fry off each piece and deep fry as you would anything else. When the bottom is golden brown, flip over. Drain on paper towels before serving.

Psst...

If you don't soak the eggplant in the salted ice water, it will turn brown. Careful not to add too much salt or your eggplant will be too salty. Because the Fish Fry contains salt, you may want to add two serving spoons of all-purpose flour to tone it down a bit before you run the eggplant through it.

Because the eggplant will cook quickly, you need to move pretty quick yourself. Once you drop the first batch of eggplant into the hot oil, you need to start the next batch in the egg and milk bowl and then the Fish Fry.

"What doesn't kill us will make us stronger."

The Wisdom of Grandma McKneely

My grandma had a collection of southern expressions like no other. While most were pretty innocent, others were a bit more poignant. What a beautiful and colorful southern lady!

If a woman was using curse words or telling a tale, my grandma would quip, "Her mouth ain't no prayer book," or "She's saying more than her prayers."

When frustrated, she could be heard whispering under her breath, "Shit and two is eight. Shit and two is eight." Does that mean shit equals six? I never did quite understand this one. When I would ask her about it, her response was always the same..."It's just an expression. I don't know where it came from."

Grandma had several expressions for the ignorant—you know—someone who doesn't know what they're talking about but says it loud and proud repeatedly. She could be heard saying, "He don't know his ass from a shotgun," or "He don't know his ass from his elbow." She was also known for "He don't know sheep shit from cotton seed," and "He don't know shit from Shineola." (Shineola was a shoe polish.)

I also learned from my grandma, "God don't like ugly and God don't sleep." Of all her expressions, I hold on most tightly to this one. "God don't like ugly." I can still hear her voice in my head when I'm ready to retaliate, get even, or just plain be ugly. My life is much easier with those words as my guide; with fewer hurt feelings and my having to make fewer apologies. The same is true for "God don't sleep." Just let your conscience be your guide.

In addition to her expressions, she shared her wisdom day-to-day. Countless times she talked me out of what I thought was a crisis. She was a calming force in my sea of chaos. In addition, she was always my coach, my mentor and my friend. Thank you, Grandma. I love you!

Maque Choux

6 ears fresh corn (shucked, washed and cut off the cob)

2 medium onions chopped

3 heaping tablespoons margarine

1 bunch green onions chopped

Tony Chachere's Original Seasoning to taste

Sauté onions in margarine on medium heat until they are transparent and beginning to turn brown. Add corn and green onions. Sauté on medium heat partially covered for 30–45 minutes; stirring often. The corn will cook down and become very tender. Add Tony Chachere's to taste.

Psst...

Don't be afraid to spice it up! If this dish is done up right, it's got a bit of a kick to it.

Some folks like to add a little bit of cream at the end. I prefer it without, but it's your call. Do what you want!

Plan on 1½–2 ears of corn per person; depending on who's at your table. It you are feeding some hungry Cajuns, you better count on two ears per person.

White corn is my favorite for this recipe. I also like to mix white and yellow corn.

"Pretty is as pretty does."
—Grandma McKneely

Warm Belly, Warm Heart

One of my favorite memories was from the time I lived with my Grandma and Grandpa McKneely. I can remember coming home from a rough day at LSU and walking into the house. The aroma of Grandma's smothered chicken shouted, "Welcome home!" The weather outside was cold, wet, and dreary, but inside my world was warm, safe, and cozy. That smell should be bottled by the air-freshener industry.

One of the great things about this comfort food is it will definitely warm your belly. Best when served hot, smothered chicken will take the chill off any night. When cooked from the heart, it will warm the hearts as well as the bellies of those at your table.

Psst...

Instead of using just the breast, you can use a fryer cut into pieces. Personally, I prefer the breast. Other folks prefer dark meat. Tailor it to meet your family's taste.

Serve in a bowl with lots of gravy. Instead of using a fork, try eating it with a spoon. The chicken can be cut with a spoon.

One of the easiest ways to dust the chicken is to place ½ cup all-purpose flour in a large Ziploc bag. Insert one piece of chicken at a time, zip the bag shut, and shake-shake-shake your booty.

This dish is great with a can of Rotel tomatoes added just after it begins to boil. Make sure you get the chopped tomatoes, though.

Sometimes I'll cheat by adding a package of brown gravy mix to darken the gravy. Add before it boils to allow time for any lumps to dissolve. Ain't nothing wrong with a few shortcuts in the kitchen.

Great leftovers! After all of the chicken has been eaten, save the gravy. It can be used as a sauce on just about any other type of meat or served over rice as a side dish.

"I love you."

Smothered Chicken

2 large onions chopped   5 stalks celery chopped fine

½ cup vegetable oil   1 cup all-purpose flour

4 bay leaves   ½ cup fresh parsley chopped

4 large chicken breasts with skin and bones

4 tablespoons Knorr Concentrated Chicken
  Flavor Broth

1 bunch green onions chopped

Tony Chachere's Original Seasoning

Fresh cracked black pepper

Chop onions and celery. Set aside for later.

Wash chicken breasts and pat dry with paper towel. Season with Tony Chachere's and lightly dust in ½ cup all-purpose flour; reserving the other ½ cup of flour for later.

In a heavy stockpot, heat oil on medium-high. Careful not to overload the pot, place one or two breasts skin-side down into the pot. Lightly brown the chicken on both sides, careful not to let it burn. Remove browned chicken from pot and continue until all four pieces are complete. Set chicken aside for later.

Add ½ cup flour to hot oil. Stir continuously until medium brown. (See roux recipe.) Once brown, add chopped onions and celery. Continue to stir and cook for two minutes. Add seven cups hot water and Knorr chicken flavor broth. Stir until roux is dissolved. Add chicken, bay leaves and chopped parsley. Bring to a boil. Lower heat to maintain rolling boil for 90 minutes, stirring occasionally. Add chopped green onions. (If the gravy gets too thick, add ¼–½ cup of hot water. Season to taste with Tony Chachere's and fresh cracked black pepper.

Serve over cooked white rice.

Mama

My mama was a mixture of Dolly Parton and Julia Sugarbaker. On one hand, she was a big-busted, full-figured petite country girl with a naiveté and charm like no other. On the other hand, she could become very spirited and share her opinions in a fiery dissertation that would make Julia proud. She was self-taught and self-made. She relied on common sense much more than book sense. She was my best friend.

While Mama had her serious side, it paled in comparison to her funny side. She loved a good laugh and would laugh for hours or even days over something she found funny. Her face would light up like a Christmas tree when she smiled. She was beautiful.

I remember our last Thanksgiving together. My sister Jodi came in from Indiana; my brother Bruce from Kentucky. We were all in the kitchen laughing at Bruce's latest faux pas when I looked at him and said, "I bet it takes you an hour and a half to watch 60 Minutes." Jodi kicked in with, "Yeah and it takes him three days to watch 48 hours." Not to be outdone, Mama quipped with, "Well, he ain't my toilet to flush." The three kids turned to Mama and collectively said, "Huh?" She said, "Well, I had to come up with something." We laughed at that expression for the rest of the Thanksgiving holiday. I still use it when someone else's business ain't any of my business.

Mama was very loving and demonstrative; with good-bye's taking about 10 minutes. First it was hugs and kisses in the house. Then hugs and kisses on the porch. Finally, she would walk me to the car for the final hugs, kisses, and "I love you." She would stand on the porch and wave as I drove away. After she died and I was leaving her house for the last time, I looked back and ached to see her waving good-bye from the porch...just one more time.

I love you Mama!

Quick and Easy Jambalaya

1 package Oak Grove Smokehouse Creole Jambalaya Mix

1 tablespoon Knorr Concentrated Chicken Flavor Broth

½ – ¾ pound smoked sausage cut into bite-size pieces

3 boneless, skinless chicken breasts cut into bite-size pieces

1 bunch green onions chopped

In a heavy saucepan, sauté sausage on medium heat until most are browning. Add chicken pieces and continue cooking until chicken is done. Add 2 ½ cups water, Knorr chicken flavor broth, and green onions. Turn heat up to high. When mixture comes to a boil, add jambalaya mix and stir. When it returns to a boil, reduce heat to simmer and cover. Cook for 20–25 minutes.

Psst...

I'd love to say Mama had a great homemade recipe for jambalaya, but she didn't. This was her version and I love it! To those of you that have shared a meal at my table and raved about the jambalaya, the secret is out...it's a doctored mix!

One bunch of green onions can be a bit much for this recipe. I usually only use the green part of the onions; discarding the white end.

If the company can handle it, I'll add some Tabasco sauce to the pot just before it begins to boil.

There are many jambalaya mixes on the market today. Taste test several of them and find the one you like the best. I like the Oak Grove Smokehouse because it's not too spicy and has a great smoky flavor.

"It's so hot in here I'm sweating like a prostitute in church."

Mama and the Squirrel

Mama lived in a quiet neighborhood that was shared with lots of critters; birds of every size, occasional armadillos, a few skunks, some possums and lots of squirrels. Lots of squirrels.

It's fine to share the neighborhood with the critters, but not your attic. Mama was often trying to track down a squirrel that had chewed his way into her attic. The first time was fun and cute. The second time was annoying. The third time was all out war!

Mama and my stepdad had different views on how to take care of the problem. Mama wanted to use the BB gun. Daddy Vic wanted a more peaceful solution. They agreed to disagree.

I'd stopped by for a visit one Sunday afternoon when I got right in the middle of the battle. Mama and I were sitting on the back patio while Daddy Vic was in the house watching the football game. Mama had just told me about the latest squirrel incident when a really big squirrel started chattering in the tree above the patio. When we looked up into the tree, there he sat; right on the lowest branch, just a fussin'. That was the last straw for Mama. She told the squirrel to wait right there that she had something for him.

Mama sneaked into the house and grabbed the BB gun without Daddy Vic seeing her. When she got to the patio, the squirrel was still there...mocking her. She pumped up the BB gun and fired a shot. She missed. The squirrel got louder. She again pumped up the BB gun and fired a shot. Again, she missed. The squirrel seemed to know he was safe. "Give me that," I said. I pumped the BB gun and fired a shot. This time the squirrel wasn't so lucky; direct hit. Just as the squirrel was falling from the tree, Daddy Vic walked onto the patio. As he watched the squirrel hit the ground, he said strongly "Mickey!" "Craig did it! It wasn't me!" she replied. There I sat, busted.

Honey-Glazed Carrots

1-pound bag baby carrots

3 tablespoons butter or margarine

6 tablespoons honey

¼ cup fresh chopped parsley

juice of ½ lemon

pinch of salt

Tony Chachere's Original Seasoning

In a medium-sized saucepan, boil carrots in water with a pinch of salt until tender. When done, drain water and put carrots in a bowl for later.

Melt butter or margarine in the same saucepan. Add honey. Stir until well blended. Add chopped parsley. Stir some more. Add boiled carrots and stir, covering all carrots with the honey mixture. Sprinkle lightly with Tony Chachere's. Squeeze the juice of ½ lemon over carrots. Stir one last time.

Cover and keep on low heat until ready to serve.

Psst...

If you'd like a little more tang, squeeze the other half of the lemon over the carrots.

This recipe is great because you can get it done ahead of the rest of the meal, put it on a back burner and forget it. Just keep it on a low heat to stay warm for up to 30–45 minutes.

"Don't start the lawnmower if you're not gonna cut the grass."

Mama's Fight

Daddy Vic died from a malignant brain tumor about a year before Mama got sick. After a brief stay in the hospital and many tests, the results were in. I was holding Mama's hand when the doctor gave her the news; lung cancer. With disbelief, we just looked at each other and held on tightly. We both cried for days.

Mama began chemotherapy right away. I was there for the first treatment; sitting on the floor next to her, holding her hand. We even found the courage to laugh at the brightly-colored crocheted afghans on the other chairs. We were both so very scared.

With her sense of humor in one hand, she fought cancer with the other. She could find humor wherever the battle led her. Even with the side effects of chemotherapy, she laughed.

A week after that first chemo appointment, I drove up to spend the weekend with her. When she answered the door, she was a mess. Her hair was falling out in handfuls. Before this, Mama would spend hours on her hair. This had to be hard for her.

"Shave my head," she said. "I can't take this anymore. Please shave my head for me." I agreed and off we went to the bathroom to take care of business. When I pulled out my electric razor, she said, "Oh, no. Use a regular razor." "Mama, I don't use a regular razor on my face, much less your head. If I nick you and you start bleeding, I'll pass out and you'll be on your own." She agreed.

My mama was beautiful without hair. Although she bought a few wigs, around the house she went ala natural. When two Girl Scouts knocked on her door selling cookies, Mama forgot about the wig. When she opened the door, the looks on their faces said it all. "What's the matter? Ain't you ever seen a bald-headed woman before?" We all laughed together. Mama bought 10 boxes that day.

Sweet Macaroni and Cheese

16-ounce package of macaroni

2 cups whole milk

4 eggs

1¼ cups sugar

1 tablespoon ground cinnamon

1 pound Velveeta cheese

1 stick margarine

Boil macaroni as directed. Do not overcook. Drain and set aside.

Preheat oven to 350°.

In a large mixing bowl, combine milk, eggs, cinnamon and sugar. Mix well until eggs are beaten and sugar dissolved. (The mixture will be runny. That's OK.)

In a casserole dish, layer macaroni, pads of margarine, and thin slices of cheese. The final layer should have cheese covering the top. Pour the egg mixture over the top layer of cheese.

Bake at 350° for 35–45 minutes; until the cheese browns. Allow to sit for 15 minutes before serving.

Psst...

Use the type of pasta you like. My favorite is the mini penne. It's just like the larger penne with the hole in the middle and cut at an angle on both ends, but a smaller version. If you like elbow macaroni, go for it. You can even let one of the kids pick their favorite pasta.

If you don't have a casserole dish, use a 9 x 9 baking pan, sheet cake pan, or a deep dish pie pan. Improvise! Just make sure it's deep.

Aunt Joe Ann, thanks for your help with this recipe. I love you!

"In the battle of good and evil, the one you feed will always win."

Mama's Side Effects

There are many side effects to chemotherapy; nausea, hair loss, loss of appetite, etc. One of the worst is really bad gas. I mean _really_ bad gas. Mama's gonna cut cartwheels in her grave for me telling this story, but here goes.

Mama and one of her sisters, Bonnie, went to Wal-Mart's tent sale in the Wal-Mart parking lot. They both loved a good bargain and were ready to shop. As they were roaming around the tent together, Bonnie heard an all too familiar sound. "Oh no, Mickey. You ain't killing me!" she said. Bonnie quickly went shopping in the opposite direction.

As Mama continued to look around, smelling that horrid smell, she watched as a man carrying an infant walked into the "fog." Mama said the look on that man's face was priceless. He literally froze in his tracks and began sticking his finger into the baby's diaper; checking for a mess. Unable to find anything, he continued to check in disbelief. Mama started laughing hysterically. That poor baby got blamed for Mama's gas.

Mama had several wigs and named each of them. Her favorite was Little Ricky. We were driving down the interstate after her latest chemo appointment. It was August in Baton Rouge and hot; really hot. When she couldn't take the heat any longer, she pulled Little Ricky from her head and began to wipe her face with it. The trucker next to us almost wrecked his rig as he watched this lady pull off her hair. We laughed all the way home about the look on his face.

Mama used her sense of humor to keep going. Chemotherapy, radiation, medication, and hospitals were exhausting. She once said she had to keep fighting because she was all her kids had left. For her courage and determined fight, I say, "Thank you, Mama."

Red Beans and Beer

1 pound dried red kidney beans	2 bottles or cans of beer
2 onions chopped	2 tablespoons margarine
½ cup chopped fresh parsley	4 bay leaves
1 pound smoked sausage cut into pieces	1 bunch green onions chopped

3 tablespoons Knorr Concentrated Chicken Flavor Broth

Tony Chachere's Original Seasoning

Tabasco Sauce

The night before cooking the red beans—sort through the bag of beans and remove any "bad" ones. In a large bowl, combine the dried beans and two bottles of beer. Soak overnight.

The following morning, pour off excess beer from the beans. In a large pot, sauté onions in margarine until transparent. Add beans and enough water to cover the beans plus two inches. Add Knorr chicken flavor broth and bay leaves. Stir until the broth is dissolved. Add sausage and bay leaves. Bring to a boil. Continue to boil for 30 minutes uncovered. Lower heat to simmer and cook covered for one hour; stirring occasionally. (If the level of liquid drops below the level of beans, add more water.) Add green onions. Continue to cook uncovered until creamy; 30 minutes to an hour. Add Tabasco sauce and Tony Chachere's to taste. Serve over cooked white rice.

Psst...

For the best pot of beans, cook the sausage whole on the grill, then cut into pieces and add it to the pot.

Don't be afraid to experiment with the meat. Add smoked ham hocks, pickle meat, or ham seasoning if you like. "Just live your life!" Whatever makes you happy will make your beans happy.

"We are not human beings trying to learn to be spiritual, but instead spiritual beings trying to learn to be human."

I Wasn't Ready

Mama's fight with cancer was going well. She was in good health and looking forward to my baby sister's wedding. Mama, a licensed florist, worked hard to prepare the flowers for Jodi's big day. Mama also had her beautiful cream-colored gown ready for the occasion. Everything was going great.

Mama went to the oncologist's office Thursday morning for a checkup. She was doing fine and he'd see her after the wedding. Because Mama had an incredible fear of flying, and the wedding was in Indianapolis, Jodi drove all night to Baker, Louisiana to pick up Mama and turn around to drive back to Indianapolis the next day. They arrived in the early hours on Sunday morning; Easter Sunday. A few hours later, she was dead…congestive heart failure.

I can still remember the phone call with my brother, Bruce. In complete disbelief and shock, it took me several times hearing the story for it to finally hit me. I immediately shifted into my "big brother mode"...I'll take care of it! Although Mama refused to fly in her lifetime, within 36 hours of her death, she was on a plane coming home.

I arrived at the funeral home a few hours early to drop off Mama's rosary. To my surprise, the funeral director took me into the room where she was to be waked. There she was...at peace. She was beautiful in her cream-colored gown she had chosen for the wedding. There were two things wrong. Her make-up was not right and Mama wouldn't be that dressed up without Shalimar perfume. After a quick trip to her house, I returned to my mama's side. As my hands trembled and my eyes cried, I reapplied her make-up. It was the last thing I could ever do for her. With a few sprays of Shalimar, she was now ready to meet God.

I wasn't ready for her to go. I love and miss you so much, Mama!

German Chocolate Upside-Down Cake

1½ sticks butter

2 8-ounce packages Philadelphia Cream Cheese

1½ pounds powdered sugar

1 cup chopped pecans

1 cup sweetened, shredded coconut

1 box Duncan Hines Moist Deluxe
   German Chocolate cake mix

1¼ cups water

3 large eggs

1 cup vegetable oil

Preheat oven to 350°.

In a saucepan, melt butter and cream cheese on medium-low heat. Once melted, slowly add powdered sugar while stirring. When completely blended, set aside for later.

Sprinkle pecans and coconut in the bottom of a 13 x 9 pan.

Mix cake mix, water, vegetable oil, and eggs per instructions on the box. Pour cake mix over pecans and coconut.

Gently pour butter, cream cheese and powdered sugar mixture over the cake mix.

Bake 40–45 minutes.

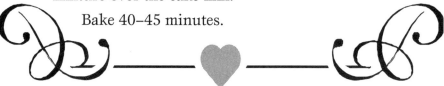

Psst...

This recipe is so easy and yet so incredibly good. The cake is rich, gooey and flat-out decadent. Pop a piece in the microwave for a few seconds, sit down with a big glass of milk and enjoy yourself Baby!

Aunt Joe Ann's son-in-law Paul shared this recipe with her. She passed it on to me. Thank both of you for sharing! This cake is almost as sweet as my Aunt Joe Ann.

"Be so real that it's unreal."

Grandma Roy

My mama's mama was a piece of work. She was 100% Cajun and quite a handful. A full-figured petite, she was known for one colorful expression every time the kitchen got too crowded... "This kitchen is wide as my ass!" Translation—"Get out!" Even the little kids knew to scatter like cockroaches when they heard those words coming from the kitchen.

The good news is her heart was also that big. She was a very loving woman and loved a good laugh. She loved telling this story about me at every family gathering.

Because I was the first grandchild on Mama's side of the family, I spent a lot of time at Grandma Roy's house. Just knee-high to a grasshopper, and in the process of potty training, I told my Grandma, "Apoo Mawmaw. Apoo." She rushed me to the bathroom and threw me on the toilet. "Apoo Mawmaw.

Apoo." She replied, "Well boy, do your business." This continued for about 30 minutes. Frustrated and unsuccessful, she removed me from the toilet and dressed me. As we walked past the dining room table, I pointed to the bowl of fruit and said, "Apoo Mawmaw. Apoo." You guessed it! All I wanted was an apple. God, how she loved telling that one on me.

Grandma Roy was also diabetic. While her diabetes was never that serious, she had her heath issues. Although she was supposed to control it with diet, she strayed many many times. Eagle Brand Condensed Milk was her favorite detour. One of the things I learned from her was to eat condensed milk instead of maple syrup. Pancakes, biscuits, waffles, and beignets are all better with condensed milk. This is the ultimate comfort food. Once in a while, I'll still bake a batch of biscuits and crack open a can of condensed milk.

To you with love, Grandma Roy!

Biscuits and Condensed Milk

1 can Pillsbury Grands! Buttermilk Biscuits
1 can Eagle Brand Condensed Milk
Margarine

Cook biscuits per directions on the package. Add margarine while biscuits are still hot.

Using an old-fashioned can opener, open the can of condensed milk three times—three punches—on one side of the lid and one little hole directly across. (This is to let air in and the thick condensed milk out.)

Pour condensed milk onto a plate. Place two or three biscuits around the edges of the condensed milk. Start sopping and enjoy!

Psst...

I'd love to say that Grandma had an incredible recipe for homemade biscuits, but she didn't. It was either canned biscuits or, on special occasions, Bisquick biscuits per the directions on the box.

Eagle Brand Condensed Milk is not the same as Pet Milk or Evaporated Milk. Please don't confuse them.

This is not rocket science, but it is the ultimate comfort food.

Because the condensed milk is so rich, I like to drink iced-water with it. This helps clear the palette for the next bite.

Condensed milk is also great on pancakes, waffles, fried biscuits, and beignets. A peanut butter and condensed milk sandwich ain't bad eating either.

"This kitchen is wide as my ass!"
—*Grandma Roy*

Grammy

In high school, I worked for Mr. and Mrs. Billy Davis at Davis' Bar-B-Q. This job served two very important purposes for me. First, it afforded me the income necessary to not be dependent on my family. Secondly, and most importantly, it was a way to escape some of the abuse at home.

The Davis' grandchildren always called them Daddy Bill and Grammy. My co-worker Bogey and I thought that if it worked for them, then it would work for us too. They never seemed to mind at all.

While working for Grammy, she sensed something at home just wasn't quite right. She tried her best to find out the truth, but the secrets were just too painful to share with anyone. She finally surrendered and told me when I was ready to talk about it, she would be there to listen. It took many years before I could take her up on that offer.

There's a very special quality about her family...her family is my family. From her daughter Donna, to her grandkids Krystal and Billy Joe, to Krystal's husband Brock and now their daughter Holland, I've been included in every family event for the past 25 years.

I remember Grammy sharing with me a conversation she had with Grandpa McKneely. This was shortly after Grandma Roy died of cancer and Mama and Grandma McKneely were soon to follow. Out of the blue, he called one night and asked if she would help look after me because very soon I wouldn't have anyone left. She promised she would always be there for me and she's lived up to that promise very well. For 25 years now, Grammy has been a constant friend and companion. She has accompanied me to every family funeral, shared her endless wisdom, and often reminded me of my humble beginnings.

I love you, Grammy!

Grammy's Strawberry Cake

¾ cup vegetable oil

½ cup water

1 tablespoon all-purpose flour

4 eggs

1 box Duncan Hines Moist Deluxe White Cake Mix

1 small box strawberry Jell-O (3 ounces)

½ cup frozen and drained strawberries

Preheat oven to 350°.

In a mixing bowl, combine cake mix, flour, Jell-O, vegetable oil, water and strawberries. (Use only the strawberries. Save the juice for later.) Mix with an electric mixer; adding one egg at a time.

Bake in two nine-inch cake pans for 25–30 minutes. Remove from oven and place on rack to cool. Once completely cooled, poke holes in each cake layer. Drizzle sweetened strawberry juice over each layer.

Strawberry Icing

¼ pound butter at room temperature

1 pound sifted powdered sugar

½ cup frozen and drained strawberries

In a large mixing bowl, slowly add the sifted powdered sugar to the butter while mixing. Then add the strawberries. Mix well and spread over the cake layers. Add a little more butter or strawberry juice if you need to make it easier to spread.

Psst...

This cake is incredible. Wow! If you really want to make it special, make it a three-layer cake by doubling the recipe. The extra batter can be used to make cupcakes for the kids. Thank you, Grammy.

Debbie: My Friend, My Mirror

I met Debbie in 1990 while volunteering for Louisiana Special Olympics. We learned very quickly we could work hard and have a great time doing it...as long as we did it together.

That was just the beginning. We seemed to click like we'd been best friends forever. In the passing years, we have literally cried on each other's shoulders too many times to count. We've laughed until we've cried and we've laughed to keep from crying. We've shared in each other's celebrations as well as been there to pick up broken pieces. Oh, the phone bills!

Debbie's a natural beauty. She's as at home at a family crawfish boil as she is rubbing elbows with the hoity-toity at a formal Mardi Gras ball; although she's the first to admit she's much more comfortable at the crawfish boil. As beautiful as she is on the outside, her soul is even more beautiful.

One of the greatest lessons I've learned from Debbie has been the importance of having a mirror you can count on to be brutally honest. Oh, I don't mean the one in the bathroom that makes your ass look big, but the human kind. A mirror that would ask why you would do something when you know it's not in your loving best interest. Why do you continue to make the same mistakes when you said you learned that lesson last time? Why do you continue to tell yourself things that you would whoop the crap out of anyone else if they said those things to you? We've been each other's mirror many times and are still best friends. Without our incredible bond, that would be impossible.

This is Debbie's favorite recipe for crawfish etouffee. She got it from her friend Jeanne Elizardi of Metairie, Louisiana. Thank you Jeanne for sharing. On the phone, Debbie answers to Debbie-Do, Grace, and Amnesia, but it's all the same... I love you, Debbie!

Crawfish Etouffee

1 pound crawfish tails

1 stick butter

1 large onion chopped

1 large bell pepper chopped

1 stalk celery chopped

1 clove garlic minced

1 tablespoon tomato paste

1 bay leaf

1 teaspoon Dijon mustard

2 teaspoons lemon juice

2 teaspoons lemon zest

4 green onions chopped

Tony Chachere's Original Seasoning

½ cup fresh parsley chopped

Melt butter and sauté onion, bell pepper, celery, garlic and bay leaf until tender; around 15–20 minutes, stirring frequently. Add crawfish tails, mustard, tomato paste, lemon zest, and lemon juice. Stir. Add Tony Chachere's Original Seasoning to taste. Cook covered for five minutes. A few minutes before serving, add green onions and parsley. Stir into the mixture and replace the lid.

Serve over cooked white rice.

Psst...

This etouffee recipe is a little more complicated than a more traditional one, but the results are well worth it. Wow!

If you prefer a little more "juice" to your etouffee, add ½ cup of chicken broth or ½ cup white wine.

Let me say it again, I love you Debbie!

"The grass is not greener on the other side; it's greener on the side you fertilize. Take care of your own backyard and nothing else will look good to you."

Stuck on Stupid!

For the first 30 years of my life, I was stuck on stupid! I spent every waking moment trying to please, impress and win over everyone else. My life was consumed by seeking love and approval of every person to cross my path. It was not only futile, but also exhausting.

Debbie and her magic mirror got me past stupid. She would hold that damn mirror right in my face and ask me "Why?" time and time again. You only have to hit me in the head with a rock twenty or thirty times before I begin to understand that it hurts. With her persistence, I finally learned the lesson. While I was so obsessed with trying to make everyone else like me, I'd never learned to like myself.

If you don't love yourself, why would you expect anyone else to? If you aren't good to yourself, then why would anyone else be? If you aren't respectful of yourself, why would you expect anyone else to be either? People typically treat you the way you let them and it's usually an indication of how you feel about yourself.

All this being said, love yourself. I mean _love_ yourself, Baby! Love is a verb; an action word. Don't just sit on your butt and think you're done. Get up and treat yourself with the same respect and generosity that you treat those _you_ love. Be good to you. Get your hair done, your nails done, take a bubble bath, take yourself to lunch. Accept your body; fat, warts and all. Cook yourself a great meal and enjoy it by candlelight. Use the good dishes. One of the things Debbie admires most about me now is I cook big meals just for myself. Sure, cooking for two, three or ten is a lot more fun, but if you can't do it for yourself then you're telling yourself you aren't worth the effort. Bull! Get in your kitchen, beat those pots and pans, and cook yourself a great meal...from your heart. Who is more deserving of your love?

You _are_ worth it Baby, I promise!

Tarragon Chicken

1 fresh fryer cut into pieces

3 tablespoons dried tarragon

2 tablespoons dried rosemary

1 onion sliced

1 heaping tablespoon Knorr Chicken Flavor Broth Concentrate

1 cup hot water

Tony Chachere's Original Seasoning

Preheat oven to 350°.

Arrange chicken pieces in the bottom of a dutch oven. Arrange onion slices between pieces of chicken. Sprinkle a generous amount of Tony Chachere's Original Seasoning across chicken. Sprinkle tarragon and rosemary across chicken. In a measuring cup, dissolve Knorr chicken flavor broth in one cup of hot water. Pour mixture over chicken.

Bake covered at 350° for 90 minutes. (Do not lift the lid during this time.) At the end of 90 minutes, remove lid and broil at 400° until brown; 30–40 minutes.

Psst...

You don't have to use a whole chicken for this recipe. If your family only likes white meat, use only breasts; dark meat, use only legs and thighs. Don't use boneless, skinless chicken for this one.

The chicken with be incredibly tender and juicy.

"God gave you your relatives, but he let you choose your friends."

Faye

I had the good fortune of meeting Faye while we both worked for Hibernia Bank. She was a customer service representative then and later promoted to customer service trainer. While working with her in the training department, I immediately admired and respected her talents. It wasn't until a few years later that I learned of her past. It was then that I truly admired and respected her character.

There are many facets to Faye. She is a beautiful African-American woman. She has a natural ability to connect with those around her. She is extremely articulate. She has a contagious belly laugh. She is a devote Christian and very active in her church. She is an unwed mother that was once on welfare.

When she shared her life story with me, I cried. Unmarried and ready to terminate her pregnancy, she found herself sitting in a clinic. She received a message saying, "Don't do it." She walked out of the clinic and kept her baby. This was truly a rough period in her life. While on welfare, she knew she wanted more for her daughter and for herself. She picked herself up and landed a job at the bank. She has continued to blossom since. I am so proud of you, Faye!

Faye and I have had so many laughs together it's impossible to keep track. Many of the laughs were while working. Repeatedly, she's asked me, "Are you gonna be stupid all your life?" We've played practical jokes on each other like no other. We've argued, fussed and fought, but our friendship was never in question. While she looks to me as a mentor, I look to her as an inspiration. You go, Girl!

Faye's life is truly a rags-to-riches story. She's living proof that with faith and hard work, you can and _will_ succeed in this life. She taught me, "God may not come when you want him, but he's always right on time." Thanks for the lesson. I love you, Faye!

Homemade Chicken Pot Pie

2 ready-made deep-dish pie shells (room temperature)

1 can Campbell's Condensed Cream of Mushroom soup

1 can Campbell's Condensed Cream of Chicken soup

16 oz. bag frozen mixed vegetables

2–3 boneless, skinless chicken breasts cut into bite-size pieces

Tony Chachere's Original Seasoning

Preheat oven to 350°.

In a large mixing bowl, combine both cans of soup, vegetables, and chicken. Stir well.

With a fork, poke several holes in the bottom of one of the pie shells. Add mixture to that pie shell. Lightly sprinkle the top of the mixture with Tony Chachere's. Gently remove the second pie shell from its pie tin and use it to cover the first one. (It's very important that the pie shell be at room temperature.) Pinch the edges of the two pie shells with your fingers; sealing the edge. Using a sharp knife, cut 5–6 short slits in the top crust. Bake for 90 minutes; until the top is golden brown and the insides are bubbly.

Psst...

Make sure you use deep-dish pie shells. The regular ones just aren't deep enough to hold the mixture.

Use the vegetable combination you like. Because I don't eat green peas, you can best believe there are no green peas in my chicken pot pie. Pick the vegetables that you and your family love to eat.

You can substitute a can of Cream of Celery soup instead of one of the others. It's a matter of personal taste.

I've even added a few peeled shrimp to this dish and loved it.

"I judged myself for not being perfect and I realized that I already am."

Hope's Favorite

Hope, a dear friend in New Orleans, loves my garlic bread; although she's not crazy about the recipe. She prefers I make a big batch of it and bring it to her. She claims it's just not the same when she makes it. (I think she likes me making it for her.)

Hope and I met many years ago at the bank. She is the epitome of femininity; not to mention beauty. She's also been a true friend for those many years. She has literally pulled me out of a manhole in the French Quarter. (That's another story.) When my mom died, she comforted me like only someone who had already endured such pain could. She is a true friend that touches not only your life and your heart, but also your soul. I love you, Hope!

As I write, "I love you, Hope," I am reminded of the many times I either tried to flatter her or just plain flirt. Each and every time, she would roll her eyes, look over her shoulder and yawn; patting her mouth with her hand like a true southern belle. It's become somewhat of a trademark of our conversations through the years. Maybe I should say, "I love you <u>anyway</u>, Hope!"

OK...about the manhole. After having dinner in the French Quarter—and not an ounce of alcohol between us—we were walking back to the car. I had Sandy on my left and Hope on my right. We were walking down the street with my arms over the shoulders of both of them. Again, Stonewall Jackson sober, we were making fun of a drunk on the other side of the street stumbling into the stoops. All of a sudden, I found myself face down in the pavement; my leg stuck knee-deep in a hole. It seems the manhole cover was missing and I fell into it. As Hope and Sandy were asking if I was OK, all I could say was, "Get me out of this hole. There might be a rat chewing on my foot!"

That story ended with x-rays at Ochsner Clinic.

Garlic Bread

2/3 cup margarine at room temperature

8-ounce container Kraft Grated Parmesan Cheese

2 teaspoons crushed garlic

2 tablespoons dried parsley

pinch of salt

Allow margarine to soften to room temperature. (Do not melt.) Add crushed garlic, dried parsley and pinch of salt. Stir well. Add grated parmesan cheese. Stir well. The mixture should have the consistency of a thick pancake batter. Refrigerate for several hours.

Before serving, allow it to become room temperature again. Slice fresh French bread, Italian bread, or any fresh crusty bread with a soft center down the side. Spread mixture on both halves and broil open-faced at 350° until golden brown.

Psst...

This is much better if you mix it a day or two ahead and allow it to sit in the refrigerator. The flavors really come together.

The mixture will keep in the refrigerator for several weeks. The danger is that you will be putting in on any piece of bread you can find; hot dog buns, hamburger buns, even leftover biscuits.

You can use more or less garlic; depending on your taste. You can also use chopped garlic instead of crushed.

Be careful when the bread is under the broiler. I've thrown away the first batch many a time because I let it burn.

My favorite bread for this recipe is Italian bread covered with sesame seeds...just a personal preference. This is true comfort food. Enjoy!

"Save the masks for Mardi Gras.
Show me who you really are."

Thanksgiving with Gary Coleman

I met Gary in 1992 at the Louisiana Special Olympics State Summer Games in New Orleans. As Chairman of Celebrities, it was my job to secure a celebrity to attend the games, make public appearances and conduct media events promoting the event. Gary Coleman was my choice and a perfect one at that. The athletes loved him. The media loved him. Gary did not miss one photo opportunity nor did he miss shaking an extended hand. He was incredible. Thank you Gary!

His manager, Dion Mial, accompanied Gary on the trip. We had such a great time that we have remained friends through the years. When I moved to San Diego in November of 1997, I knew no one there. With Thanksgiving just two weeks away, Dion invited me to his grandma's house in Los Angeles for dinner. Gary would also be there.

Because my grandma taught me you never show up empty-handed, I asked what I could bring. "Just your appetite," was Dion's response. My grandma would cut cartwheels in her grave if I showed up with nothing. My pork roast had always been a success, so why not.

First of all, Dion's grandma was the most genteel and loving lady I'd ever met. What a beauty! She welcomed this country boy into her home and quickly put me to work in the kitchen. I love you, Blanche!

As the family sat down to dinner, with tables set up throughout the house, we began an incredible feast. This feast not only fed my tummy, but my heart as well. There was so much love around the house that I couldn't help but be enveloped by it. Wow!

From the next room, I heard Gary say, "Craig, this pork roast is kickin' off the table!" I turned to Dion to ask, "Is that a good thing?" Dion smiled his Cheshire cat grin and said, "Oh yeah." "Thank you Gary," I replied. From that moment on, the pork roast has been known as the "Kickin' Off the Table" pork roast.

"Kickin' Off the Table" Pork Roast

4–6 pound bone-in Boston butt pork roast

1 can Coke, Dr. Pepper, or Sprite (do not use diet)

1 cup chicken broth

2 medium onions chopped

3 stalks celery chopped

3 bay leaves

Tony Chachere's Original Seasoning

Preheat oven to 350°.

Rub pork roast with Tony Chachere's seasoning. Place into a dutch oven. Mix chopped onions and celery together. Pack as much of the mixture on top of the roast as you can with your hands. Any extra, just scatter around the roast. Add chicken broth and soda around the roast; not to disturb the celery and onion mix on top. Add bay leaves to the liquid. Cover dutch oven with lid. Bake at 350° for 3½–4 hours.

Psst...

The first two hours, do not open the lid at all. Cook covered for a total 3 hours. At that time, remove the lid, knock the seasoning mixture into the liquid, baste, and cook an additional 30–60 minutes; allowing the liquids to reduce and the roast to brown. You may want to raise the temperature to 400° or switch from bake to broil.

The roast will be fork tender and fall off the bone. Don't try to slice it with a knife.

Heated leftovers are great served on sandwiches.

To those that cannot live without garlic, add garlic! You can even stuff the roast with garlic and the seasoning mixture before cooking.

"What we want the most is what we are most afraid of."

Mark's Heart

Mark is one of my dearest friends in San Diego. He had a friend with a timeshare in Palm Springs and they invited me to go with them for the weekend. Although I was going through a severe period of insomnia, I agreed. My first trip to Palm Springs. I was too excited!

There were four of us in the one-bedroom condo; Greg, Mark and his date, and myself. I was sharing the Murphy bed with Greg while Mark and his date got the bedroom. After a great dinner, we decided to call it a night. Greg stayed behind for a nightcap. As I was crawling into bed, Mark said he and his date were going for a walk. Cool. The condo all to myself and sleep just minutes away!

Just as I dozed off, I was awakened by the slamming of the front door. All I wanted was sleep. Again, just as I dozed off, the door opened and slammed again. Damn! About 10 minutes later, Mark walked in and announced he was going for a ride. Good! Just as I dozed off yet a third time, the front door opened and slammed shut.

Mark plopped down next to me on the Murphy bed and said he'd just been dumped. I was more interested in sleep than his social life at the time. "Are you sure?" I asked hesitantly. (If he were dumped that night, surely he would still be dumped in the morning.) "I think I would know if I was dumped," he replied as he began to cry.

I sat up and started to comfort this 6'1" Navy officer. As his tears began rolling down my chest, I began to cry with him. (I have a rule that nobody cries alone.) "What's wrong with me? Why can't I find someone?" he asked. I replied, "Mark, the only problem with you is your heart's as big as my ass." Through his tears, he looked at me and said, "I wish you had a smaller ass." I looked at him and said, "You're not the first person to say that to me." Through the tears, we laughed hysterically. I love you, Mark!

"The Best" Shrimp Dip

4 cans broken shrimp

3 pounds headless shrimp (boiled, peeled, de-veined and broken into thirds)

½–1 quart mayonnaise

1 bunch green onions chopped

Tony Chachere's Original Seasoning

Tabasco Sauce

Rinse and drain canned shrimp. Soak in ice water for 15 minutes. Drain. Add mayonnaise—enough to break up the shrimp and make a loose paste. Stir well. (In New Orleans, this is called shrimp butter and is great on crackers.) Add boiled shrimp. Stir some more. Add chopped green onions. Stir again. Add Tony Chachere's and Tabasco to taste. Stir yet again. Allow to chill for a few hours before serving. Serve with fancy crackers—preferably those that won't break when you dip.

Psst...

When serving this dip, I like to completely cover the top with a thin layer of Tabasco Sauce. For those weak at heart, wait until the first layer is eaten before you start dipping.

If the boiled shrimp aren't quite as spicy as you would like, add Tony Chachere's. Allow them to sit a few minutes in a generous sprinkling before adding to the mixture. By breaking the boiled shrimp into thirds, it makes them go farther and makes it easier to dip.

Should you ever have any leftovers, this makes a great sandwich on fresh French bread with a little mayonnaise and a lot of lettuce.

If you like raw onion, add raw onion. It's your party; have fun!

"Denial is a wonderful place to live, but the rent is expensive."

Family Traditions

Family traditions are so very important. They can help define holidays and family history. Think about some of your own family traditions and how meaningful they are to you.

One of my favorite traditions is the family gumbo on Christmas Eve. In our family, it was long a tradition to always eat gumbo on Christmas Eve. As we kids got older, Mama amended the tradition to the one that I fondly remember today.

Mama would start making the gumbo in the afternoon. Once she got the roux done and the gumbo started, she would let it simmer for the rest of the day. Each of us kids was assigned to bring one of the meat ingredients. I was always the shrimp. My sister Jodi was usually the chicken. My brother Bruce was always the oysters. (Because if he forgot, it was no big deal since he and Mama were the only two that liked them anyway.) As we arrived on Christmas Eve, we made our contributions to the pot. It became the family gumbo.

This tradition is still so strong in me that I introduced it to my in-laws in California. Each Christmas Eve, we made gumbo as a family; one peeling shrimp, one making the roux, one chopping vegetables, etc. To be honest, it's one of the few things I miss about my ex.

I challenge you to carry on existing traditions with your family and even create a few new ones of your own. When loved ones are gone, it's memories like traditions that you can hold on to tightly.

Family Gumbo

1 cup vegetable oil

1½ cup all-purpose flour

3 medium or 2 large onions

5 stalks celery

1 bunch green onions chopped

½ cup chopped fresh parsley

2 heaping tablespoons gumbo filé

5 bay leaves

6 tablespoons Knorr Concentrated
   Chicken Flavor Broth

1 pound smoked sausage cut into
   bite-size pieces

3–4 boneless, skinless chicken breasts
   cut into bite-size pieces

3–4 pounds headless shrimp peeled and
   de-veined

Tony Chachere's Original Seasoning

Fresh cracked black pepper

Tabasco Sauce

Chop onions and celery. Set aside for later.

In a heavy 8-quart pot, make a roux using the vegetable oil
and flour. (See roux recipe.) When the roux is deep brown and
done, add chopped onions and celery. Stir mixture well. Allow
to cook two minutes before adding 12 cups hot water. Add Knorr
chicken flavor broth and stir well; dissolving roux and broth in

water. Turn heat up to high and bring to a boil. (Careful not to let it boil over.) When it reaches a boil, lower heat to medium. Add bay leaves and sausage. Continue with a rolling boil and stir every few minutes. After boiling 45 minutes, add chicken and parsley. Lightly season with Tabasco, Tony Chachere's, and cracked black pepper. (You'll add more later.) After 30 minutes, add shrimp and green onions. Continue cooking for 5 minutes. Add Tony Chachere's, Tabasco sauce and cracked black pepper to taste. Turn off heat. Sprinkle gumbo filé across the gumbo and cover pot with the lid. Do not open the pot for 20 minutes.

Skim off any grease and serve over cooked white rice.

Psst...

Baby, you can put in your gumbo whatever YOU like; bell pepper, oysters, jumbo lump crabmeat, crawfish, okra, etc. In the old days, gumbo was a cheap way of feeding a lot of people with whatever you had on hand. Experiment and have fun with it. You can do it, I promise!

"Dreams really do come true."

Cajun Christmas

Besides having gumbo on Christmas Eve, there were a few other traditions celebrated on Mama's side of the family during the holidays.

Every year, Grandma Roy made Christmas candy. The Christmas balls were my favorite. There was also an unspoken ritual when it came to eating. The children ate first so when they left the table, they went outside to play. Then, the men ate so they could watch the football games after leaving the table. Last at the table were the women so they could sit and visit before doing the dishes. (Sounds pretty sexist when you think about it.) I usually started with the men and stayed through with the women. And don't think the women did without anything after all the others had first pick. They kept a stash of every dish in the oven just for their seating at the table.

Another tradition was Grandma Roy's story about stuffing the turkey. It seems when I was a little boy, she told me the turkey was stuffed with toilet paper. As a young kid, I was amazed every year to discover the toilet paper was gone when the turkey was carved. I was about 13 before I realized she was only joking, but how she loved to tell that story every Christmas. I love you, Grandma!

Although Mama and Grandma Roy are now celebrating the holidays together in Heaven, those homemade family traditions still warm my heart every year. As I prepare my own turkey for the oven, I smile thinking about stuffing the bird with toilet paper. While making the Christmas balls, I think about how as a kid I would sneak a few in my pocket before going outside to play. Those loving traditions define the holidays for me.

I invite you to take a look at your own holiday traditions and ask yourself what you're doing to keep them alive. Don't let them die. I'd also like to invite you to create new ones. Go for it. Make it happen!

Grandma Roy's Christmas Balls

2 pounds powdered sugar

1 can Eagle Brand Condensed Milk

1 bag sweetened coconut (7 ounces)

1 cup finely chopped pecans

1 stick butter at room temperature

3 bags milk chocolate chips

Mix powdered sugar, condensed milk, coconut, chopped pecans and butter together. (Do not cook.) Mix very well and shape into small balls. Set on wax paper and chill for an hour or more.

In a double boiler or microwave, melt 3 bags real milk chocolate chips. Dip balls in the melted chocolate. (A tablespoon is very helpful with this.) Place on wax paper in a cool location to harden the chocolate.

Psst...

Careful when you are mixing the ingredients. The mixture will be pretty stiff and can burn up your mixer if you aren't careful.

It's much easier to roll the mixture into balls if your hands are wet. Resist the temptation to "hurry up" by making the balls too big.

I prefer to put a whole nut in the center of each ball...almonds, cashews, macadamias. You know, the salted ones in the can.

The back of the chocolate chip bag should have directions for melting; either double boiler or microwave. Make sure you get milk chocolate chips, not bittersweet chocolate or baking chips.

My grandma was known for adding a few tablespoons of rum to the mixture to make rum balls. If you do, keep them away from the kids.

*"Don't spit in the well.
You may have to drink."*

"The" Potato Salad Recipe

This potato salad has been invited to parties I haven't. I've also been told if I couldn't attend a particular party, make sure to send the potato salad in my place. It's that good!

While the recipe can appear to be a bit intimidating, it's really pretty easy. It's just a matter of getting everything ready before the mixing begins. It also takes work to stir the mixture, but you can do it.

This is an incredible comfort food. Enjoy!

Psst...

I don't particularly like egg yolks, so I only use six yolks in my potato salad. (I throw away the other six.) Don't chop the egg whites too small. It's best to slice them and let them break apart when mixing.

The secret to this potato salad is to make it creamy while allowing some of the potato chunks to remain. If yours is not creamy enough, stir. It may take a few minutes of working that spoon to get the desired consistency, but it's worth it. You know it's done when it looks more like a batch of lumpy mashed potatoes instead of potato salad.

Again, if you like raw onions, add chopped raw onions. If you like relish, pickles, or olives, go for it! You may also want to try one of the fancy mustards instead of regular yellow mustard.

If your doctor says you can't have bacon, get a new doctor. Seriously, try making it with turkey bacon. If you are watching your fat, use the fat-free mayonnaise. They're not quite the same, but pretty good in a pinch.

I love this potato salad served at room temperature. Other folks prefer it chilled. Try it both ways and you decide, Baby.

Cajun Country Potato Salad

5 pounds red potatoes	12 eggs
1 bunch green onions chopped	1 quart mayonnaise
1 tablespoon yellow mustard	1 pound bacon

4 tablespoons Tony Chachere's Original Seasoning

5 tablespoons Knorr Concentrated Chicken
    Flavor Broth

Tabasco Sauce

Wash potatoes. Remove any bad spots, but do not peel. Cut into cubes. (No, they don't have to all be the same size.) Place in a large stockpot with enough water to cover the potatoes. Add Tony Chachere's and Knorr chicken flavor broth. Stir. Rinse 12 eggs and place on top of the potatoes. (Make sure the water covers the eggs too.) Boil potatoes and eggs together. After about 15 minutes of boiling, remove the eggs with a large slotted spoon. Set aside for later. Continue to boil the potatoes until some are broken apart and others are still whole. Remove from heat and allow to sit in broth for at least 30–45 minutes.

Microwave bacon. It will take a few batches to cook the whole pound. Make sure the bacon is fully cooked and crispy. Crumble (not too small) and set aside. Chop green onions. Slice eggs.

When the potatoes have cooled, pour off excess broth. Do not pour into a colander. (You want some of the broth with the potatoes.)

In a really large mixing bowl, combine potatoes, bacon, eggs, and green onions. Stir. Stir some more. Add mayonnaise—start with about ½ to ¾ of the quart at first. Stir. Some of the potatoes will completely break apart while others retain their shape. Add about one tablespoon yellow mustard. Stir again. Add Tony Chachere's and Tabasco to taste. Don't be shy with the seasoning. If the consistency is not smooth and creamy, add a little more mayonnaise and continue stirring.

"Coulda, shoulda, and woulda . . .
Three poorly disguised excuses."

Don't Buy It!

There are a lot of salespeople out there, but don't buy the shit they're trying to sell. These folks come in every size, shape and color. They are disguised as strangers, friends, family members, bosses, co-workers and even your spouse.

If I'd bought everything they were selling, I would believe myself to be an ugly, unsuccessful, fat, stupid, useless idiot. The list goes on and on; just pick one. If you bought any of it, you believe it too.

After my first year as a Special Olympics volunteer, I called Grandma Roy to tell her about it. Jack Klugman and Larry Drake were the celebrities that year. Many of the New Orleans Saints were there as well. When I told her who I'd worked with, she told me, "Be careful. You can't get too high. You know you're just a Cajun." For the first time in my then 30 years of life, I told my grandma off. "Never

102

will I be held back because of who I am, what I am, or where I grew up!"

Had I bought what she was selling, I would have declined the opportunity to be Chairman of Celebrities the following year. Had I bought what she was selling, I would have missed out on many of life's opportunities. The funny thing is this came from someone that truly loved me. She probably didn't even know what she was doing. She meant no harm, but was selling none the less. I chose not to buy it!

Think about the many salespeople that have crossed your door; trying to sell _you_ a crock of crap. How much of it did you buy? Baby, did you keep the receipt? Get rid of it and get you some new and improved things to believe about yourself. Clean out those closets and throw out those old beliefs. You are a beautiful spiritual being...perfect just as you are. Sure, there are things we'd all like to work on, but today, right now, you are perfect just as you are!

Quick Chicken and Gravy

1 tablespoon margarine

¼ cup fresh parsley chopped

6-ounce jar sliced mushrooms—drained

½ onion chopped

1 bunch green onions chopped

1 pack brown gravy mix

4 boneless, skinless chicken breasts cut into bite-size pieces

1 tablespoon Knorr Concentrated Chicken Flavor Broth

Sauté onion and mushrooms in margarine until they are beginning to brown. Add chicken. Sauté until chicken is cooked.

In a measuring cup, dissolve brown gravy mix in one cup of cold water. Stir until all lumps are gone. Pour over chicken, onion, and mushrooms. Dissolve Knorr chicken flavor broth in one cup of cold water. Pour into the pot. Add green onions and parsley. Cook at a rolling boil uncovered for 30 minutes; allowing the gravy to reduce by half or more. (The gravy should be rich and thick.)

Serve over cooked white rice.

Psst...

Because the gravy mix and chicken broth both contain salt, be careful when seasoning. It can get too salty quick. Also remember the gravy will be reduced by half. Wait until the gravy is almost done before seasoning to taste. A shot of Tabasco sauce is usually enough.

If the gravy gets too thick, add ¼–½ cup hot water.

Here's another opportunity to make it your own. If you don't like mushrooms, don't use them. Add chopped red bell pepper, garlic, etc.

"An armadillo ain't nothing but a possum on the half shell."

Love and Relationships

When it comes to love and relationships, I have two very steadfast rules. First, _never_ be with anyone that treats you worse than you treat yourself. I can do bad by myself. I don't need any help. Second, be _very_ good to yourself. Treat yourself with the same love and generosity that you treat the one you love. If you really want to get my attention, be better to me than I am to myself.

These rules not only work for romantic relationships, but also friendships. I remember a "friend" in New Orleans that was very caustic. He belittled me over and over to feel better about himself. This was fun and cute the first three hundred times. After that, I'd had it. Why would I choose a friend that would treat me that way? Finally, one day, I had to say to him, "You're outta here!"

I've also learned that there are four levels of connection in love relationships. First, and the easiest to recognize, is the physical connection. The second is the mental connection. The third is the emotional connection. Finally, there is the spiritual connection. The key to a long-lasting and powerful relationship is to find someone that is cooking <u>with</u> you on all four burners. Now that's really hot!

I think we've all had someone in our lives that we connected with physically. They were dumb as a box of rocks, but what a body! Or maybe it was someone you connected with mentally, had a strong emotional connection, but physically there was no connection. I just can't french kiss someone I don't find physically attractive.

While there are many combinations of one, two and three-burner cooking, the best is by far cooking on all four burners. Imagine it, someone that makes you melt physically, someone you respect and admire their mind, someone you love beyond words, and someone that connects with your soul. Wow! Now that's some powerful cooking!

Baked Potato Soup

2 tablespoons margarine

2 medium onions chopped

1 teaspoon dried parsley

1 stick butter or margarine

2 tablespoons Knorr Concentrated Chicken
  Flavor Broth

Tony Chachere's Original Seasoning

Salt and fresh cracked black pepper

Bacon, shredded cheddar cheese and chopped
  green onions for garnish

3 bay leaves

5 pounds red potatoes

2 cups whole milk

In a large heavy stockpot, slowly sauté chopped onions in 2 tablespoons margarine until onions begin to brown. Add six cups water and Knorr chicken flavor broth. Stir. Wash potatoes well and remove any bad spots, but do not peel. Cut potatoes into cubes and add to stockpot. Bring to a boil. Lower heat to maintain rolling boil. Boil for 45 minutes–1 hour. Remove from heat. Allow to set for 15 minutes.

Using the back of a large spoon, smash about ¾ of the potatoes against the bottom of the pot. Add one stick of butter or margarine; stirring as it melts. Slowly add two cups whole milk while stirring continuously. Season to taste. Serve in a large bowl; topped with crumbled bacon, shredded cheddar cheese and chopped green onions.

Psst...

This is not only a very hearty soup, but also one incredible comfort food. It's great on those cold, rainy days.

I love this soup with lots of bacon and cheese. You can also add a bit of sour cream if that makes you happy. It's like eating a smooth baked potato.

"Get out of your own way."

Cooking from the Heart

What's cooking from the heart look like? First, get comfortable. Put on some clothes that don't choke you around the neck or the waist. Then, start with a clean kitchen. Unload the dishwasher, clean off the counter and make some room. I hate to start cooking with a dishwasher full of dirty dishes or even worse, with dirty dishes in the sink. Take a few minutes to clean up. With the dishwasher empty, it's easy to drop in the dishes as you go, rather than letting them pile up and stare you in the face as you're trying to cook.

Next, make sure you've got everything you need before you start. Have you ever been in the middle of cooking and realized you were out of something? There is nothing worse than _that_ trip to the grocery store. Don't start until you've got all your stuff together.

Then, take your time and enjoy what you're doing. That's right, enjoy cooking. Do it with love, Baby!

Crank up the CD player with your favorite music. Sing like ain't nobody listening, even if you do make up your own words. Think about the love you have for those sitting at your table and let dinner be an expression of that love. Light a candle.

Don't be afraid to use the good dishes and the good glasses. When my mama died, she had tons of "good" stuff she was saving. Saving for what? She never got to use them. Make it fancy!

Also, cook up something for a sick or elderly friend and bring it to them. Maybe a neighbor that's alone or lonely. Have you ever been sick and someone made you a batch of soup? Remember how wonderful it tasted? Pass it on, Baby! There is nothing like homemade soup when you're sick, but you're usually too sick to make it yourself. Let's take care of each other. That other person is somebody's mama, daddy, sister, brother, aunt, uncle or child. Wouldn't you want somebody to take care of one of your relatives? Pass it on, Baby! Pass it on.

Fried Sweet Potatoes

2 tablespoons sugar
½ teaspoon cinnamon
2–3 medium sweet potatoes
Vegetable oil

Combine sugar and cinnamon in a small bowl. Stir until well mixed. Set aside for later.

Wash and peel the sweet potatoes. Slice into round medallions no thicker than ¼ – ½ ". (The thinner the slices, the more potato chip flavor. The thicker the slices, the more sweet potato flavor.)

Deep fry in vegetable oil until golden brown on both sides. Drain on paper towels. Sprinkle with cinnamon-sugar mixture. Serve hot.

Psst...

There are several varieties of sweet potatoes. While you can use the golden sweet potatoes, the orange variety is much sweeter and my favorite. Do not try this with yams.

Peeling sweet potatoes with a vegetable peeler is the only way to go. Trying to use a knife could cost you a finger or an emergency room visit. Stick with the vegetable peeler. It's safer, quicker and easier.

Because of the cinnamon-sugar, kids really seem like this dish. It's an easy way to get them to eat vegetables.

*"It's not too late, it's never
too late for love."*
—*Ariana Storm*

Giving Back

I truly believe one of the greatest tragedies in this lifetime is to leave having received more than you gave.

In my lifetime, I have received so much from so many. Some held me tenderly while picking up the shattered pieces while others were ruthless teaching valuable lessons. The truth is, where would I be without them? Where would I be without Grandma McKneely, Hattie B. Johnson, Mrs. Genius, Mike Lee, Brent-Alan Huffman or Beverly Fortenberry? Or any of the special people that took the time, love and energy to make a difference in this shy and insecure country boy's life.

Think about those in your life that really believed in you before you believed in yourself. Where would you be without those that gave so freely? Who would you be today without their fingerprints on your life? If those that gave to you are still with us, let them know how much they meant to you. Whether a teacher, coach, boss, friend, relative or parent, let them know what their giving meant to you.

We've all received. It's critical we give back. Seek out ways to give to others. This can be as simple as helping a child read a book or complimenting the elderly lady in line at the grocery store about how nice her hair looks today. Look for ways to bring a smile to the heart of someone else. I'll always remember the look on the little old lady's face when we finally found her car in the crowded parking lot. She even bent down and kissed the trunk of that old Buick!

Volunteering is an incredible way to give back. Whether it's Special Olympics, Children's Hospital, an at-risk youth program, find an organization that speaks to your heart and give. It doesn't matter who you are, you have something to offer; time, money, love or support.

I've found that nothing feels quite as good as when you give back...from the heart.

Shrimp and Crawfish Stew

1 cup vegetable oil	1 bunch green onions chopped
1½ cups all-purpose flour	1 pound peeled crawfish tails
2 medium onions chopped	4 stalks celery chopped
4 bay leaves	Tabasco sauce

4 tablespoons Knorr Concentrated Chicken Flavor Broth

2 pounds headless shrimp peeled and de-veined

Tony Chachere's Original Seasoning

In a large, heavy stockpot, heat oil on medium to medium-high heat. Add flour. Stir continuously until brown. (See roux recipe.)

When the roux is done, add chopped onions and celery. Continue to cook for two minutes. Add six cups hot water and stir until the roux is dissolved. Bring to a boil. Add Knorr chicken flavor broth, bay leaves, parsley and green onions. Lightly season with Tony Chachere's. Simmer for 45 minutes to one hour; stirring frequently. Add crawfish and shrimp. Continue to simmer for 15 minutes. Season to taste with Tony Chachere's and Tabasco sauce.

Serve over cooked white rice.

Psst...

Because of the thickness of the stew, be careful not to let it stick to the bottom and burn. Stir frequently. If the stew becomes too thick, add about ½ cup hot water.

Mama used to add diced potatoes and baby carrots to her version of this stew. This made the seafood and the stew go farther.

If you aren't a big fan of crawfish, what's wrong with you? Instead of the crawfish, this dish is great with a pound of jumbo lump crabmeat or an extra pound of shrimp.

"My beauty comes from within."

The Little Old Lady Crossing the Street

It was July in New Orleans. I was pulling out of my parking garage after a tough workout at the gym. My mama was dying of lung cancer and I was right in the middle of a pity party.

I pulled into traffic and saw a little old lady with leg braces trying to cross Rampart Street with her walker. She was scared.

I pulled my car across the three lanes to block traffic so she could cross. When she reached the neutral ground (median), she turned to me and said "thank you" through the car window. I cried all the way home thinking about how selfish humans can be at times.

A week later, I was walking to the parking garage and saw the same little old lady on that same journey. I ran to catch up with her and positioned my body between her and the oncoming traffic. I said, "Come on, Sweetie, let's cross this street." She looked up at me and slowly replied, "I can't walk fast. I wish I could." I looked at her and said, "That's OK. These cars have nowhere to go."

We slowly crossed Rampart Street. When we reached the other side, she froze. The curb was too tall and she couldn't get up there. I looked her in the eyes and said, "Together we can!" I asked her what I could do to help. She said, "Just don't let me fall." I stood behind her, holding her fragile waist, as she lifted her walker onto the sidewalk. With both hands, she lifted her left leg with the brace onto the sidewalk. She did the same with the right. As I held her steady, she lifted herself using the walker. She looked at me with such excitement. "We did it! We did it!" she said. With tears in my eyes, I said, "That's right. And together, we can do anything. Now you go on and have a nice evening." Again, I cried all the way home.

I couldn't make cancer go away, but dammit, I could help the little old lady cross the street. I felt empowered and it felt good!

"Kitchen Sink" Soup

1 tablespoon margarine	1 large onion chopped
½ cup fresh parsley chopped	4 bay leaves
6-ounce package sliced mushrooms	1 bunch green onions chopped

16-ounce package baby carrots

4 boneless, skinless chicken breasts cut into
    bite-size pieces

4 tablespoons Knorr Concentrated Chicken
    Flavor Broth

1 package Hormel Boneless Smoked Pork Chops cut
    into bite-size pieces

4 stalks celery cut into bite-size pieces

1½ pounds headless shrimp peeled and de-veined

Tony Chachere's Original Seasoning

Tabasco Sauce

In a large stockpot, sauté onions in margarine until transparent. Add eight cups water and bring to a boil. Add Knorr chicken flavor broth, bay leaves, chicken, pork chops, mushrooms, and parsley. Lightly season with Tony Chachere's. Cook on a rolling boil or heavy simmer for 45 minutes; stirring occasionally.

Add carrots, celery and green onions. Continue boiling for 15 minutes. Add shrimp and stir. Remove from heat. Cover with lid and allow to sit for 15 minutes. Season to taste with Tony Chachere's and Tabasco sauce.

Psst...

These are a few of my favorite things in soup; everything but the kitchen sink. Make it your own by combining YOUR favorite ingredients. Try adding more vegetables and/or different meats.

Depending on my mood, I sometimes add pasta noodles or frozen Chinese potstickers. Most of the time, I like it without either.

"Do all things with love."

Lessons
Learned

♥ *Grandma McKneely can color good.—age 5*

♥ *I don't eat green peas no matter how long I sit at the table.—age 7*

♥ *Silence can be deafening.—age 9*

♥ *Funerals make adults cry loud and act strange.—age 11*

♥ *Stepparents should love their stepkids as much as their own.—age 13*

♥ *Never wear pants that are too tight to the homecoming dance.—age 15*

♥ *Stop and smell the roses, live life to its fullest and tell people when you love them.—age 17*

♥ *No one should have to bury a parent at this age.—age 19*

♥ *A college degree doesn't mean instant success.—age 21*

♥ Some people will be nice to you only to get what they want.—age 23

♥ Secrets destroy relationships.—age 25

♥ Employees can move mountains when they work with you, not for you.—age 27

♥ Volunteer work does wonders for your own heart.—age 29

♥ Cancer patients are scared and want to be held.—age 31

♥ It hurts when the child becomes the parent.—age 32

♥ Losing my mom to cancer broke my heart.—age 33

♥ I'm a much better man because of my Grandma McKneely.—age 34

♥ I never want to be pitied; only envied.—age 35

♥ One candle doesn't loose any of its brightness by lighting another.—age 36

♥ Time heals, but the heart doesn't forget the pain.—age 37

♥ Never walk down the aisle with someone who isn't capable of intimacy. I still miss the loved ones that have passed on before me. Do all things with love. We are not human beings trying to learn to be spiritual, but instead spiritual beings trying to learn to be human. And finally...I still don't eat green peas.—age 39

Grammy's Coconut Cake

Duncan Hines Moist Deluxe White Cake

Prepare cake per directions on box. Remove from oven and allow to cool thoroughly.

Frosting

2 egg whites

1½ cups sugar

2 teaspoons light corn syrup
    or ¼ teaspoon cream of tartar

a cup cold water

dash salt

1 teaspoon pure vanilla extract

3–6 bags shredded, sweetened coconut
    (frozen is best)

Place egg whites, sugar, corn syrup, cold water and salt in top of a double boiler. Do not place over heat yet. Beat one minute with a mixer. Now place over boiling water and cook—beating constantly until frosting forms stiff peaks; about 7 + minutes. Do not overcook.

Remove from heat. Pour into a cool mixing bowl. Add vanilla extract and beat until frosting consistency; about two minutes. Once frosting is completely cooled, frost cake. Before the frosting sets, pack the shredded coconut over the top and sides of the cake. Enjoy!

Psst...

Grammy usually uses two boxes of cake mix and makes a three- layer cake. She also drizzles coconut milk or simple syrup flavored with coconut extract over each layer before frosting. If you do this, make sure you keep the cake in the refrigerator or it may sour.

"Before you can get it together, it first has to fall apart."

Secrets, Tips and Lagniappe

Boiling Shrimp—Adding a heaping tablespoon of butter or margarine to the water will make shrimp easier to peel. Just be careful you don't overcook the shrimp. Bring the water to a boil with the desired seasoning, lemon, onion, etc. After boiling for about 10–15 minutes, add shrimp. Turn off the heat and allow the shrimp to cook for just a few minutes. Taste to see when done. Remove from water.

Boneless, Skinless Chicken Breasts—Always wash chicken breasts under running water and dry with paper towel. Please remove any "stuff"—including fat, gristle and membrane. That "stuff" is just nasty. Cut it off and throw it away.

Breaking Bread—Once bread is on the table, never slice it. You "break" bread with friends. If you cut it at the table, it will cut the friendship.

Celery—Before you chop celery, make sure you wash it well and remove the ribs; you know, the long stringy things. If not, they can turn bitter when cooking. The easiest way I've found to remove them is to use a vegetable peeler.

Double Boiler—I have never owned a double boiler in my life. I've always used what's called a "poor man's double boiler" in my kitchen. Take a large pot and place a few cups of water in it. Turn the heat to medium-high. When the water begins to boil, use a stainless steel mixing bowl floating in the water as the "double boiler."

Dutch Oven—I love cooking in my dutch oven; also known as a covered roaster. Mine is an old hand-me-down from a great friend. It's got several dings, scrapes and chips, but Baby, can it cook! It's Granite Ware—you know—the black enamel-looking paint with white flecks all over it. Because they aren't expensive at all, every kitchen should have at least one or two.

Fresh Cracked Black Pepper—One of the best birthday presents I ever bought myself was a pepper mill. (Like you don't buy yourself birthday presents!) It's opened my eyes to what pepper is supposed to be. There is nothing like the taste of coarsely ground fresh black pepper. This is another "must have" for every kitchen.

Fresh Parsley—When using fresh parsley, remove the stems before chopping. I've always just held the stem in one hand and plucked the leaves with the other. Personally, I prefer the curly parsley. It just looks better…kinda fancy, ya know.

Giving Roses—Grandma McKneely used to say, "Give me roses while I'm living. Don't wait until I'm dead." This is so true on two levels. First, send flowers to the ones you love while they are alive and can enjoy them. (This includes buying flowers for yourself!) Secondly, and more deeply, let the ones you love know it frequently while they are living, not when they are laid out in a funeral home. I've seen too many times loved ones throwing themselves onto the casket in grief because they had so much left unsaid. It's too late then.

Green Onions—Green onions are sold in bunches, usually wrapped together with rubber bands. I typically only use the green part and throw away the white end.

Gumbo—Making great gumbo is an art. The hardest part is making the roux. Once the roux is complete, the rest is easy. Add whatever you like; chicken, sausage, shrimp, duck, etc. Gumbo is better the next day and even better on the following day. It freezes well, but don't put in the filé or okra if you plan to freeze the leftovers. For some reason, it alters the flavor.

Headless Shrimp—If shrimp have been frozen, the heads are removed. If shrimp are fresh, they're usually sold with the heads. If the recipe calls for a pound of headless shrimp and your shrimp have heads, buy a pound and a half; two pounds of headless, buy three pounds. It's better to have extra than not enough.

Housekeeping—Make your bed every morning as soon as you get out of it. That way, whether it's 10 minutes later or the rest of the day, the bed is made and it just makes you feel good when you look at it; all made and clean. Grandma McKneely taught me this many years ago and it's served me well.

Knorr Concentrated Chicken Flavor Broth—This little jewel goes into just about everything at my house. It brings a richness to any gravy, soup or gumbo. It's also the secret ingredient in my Cajun Country Potato Salad. Once you try it, you will never again use those dried out little cubes.

Okra—When you cook okra, it's gonna get slimy. Before adding it to gumbo, cook it in a separate saucepan with a little water and a capful of white vinegar. The vinegar will cut the slime. Don't overcook the okra though. When done, pour off the slimy water and add just the cooked okra to the pot of gumbo.

Onions—When the recipe calls for chopped onions, chop the onions as large or as fine as you want. Because my mama hated to see onions floating in her gravies, soups and gumbo, she insisted I chop all onions very fine. Baby, at your house, you do what you want!

Red Beans—Red beans freeze well for up to several weeks. Make a big batch and freeze individual servings for later. There is nothing like a 3-hour meal in 15 minutes. What a great treat in the middle of the week!

Rolling Boil—If you've gotten this far, you've read "rolling boil" several times by now. It's just my way of saying a fast simmer. Not an out-of-control boil, but a nice, healthy, fast simmer. I'm certainly no rocket scientist and neither is this.

Skimming Grease—Smothered chicken and gumbo, because of the oil in the roux, may need to be skimmed before serving. The easiest way to do this is to remove the pot from heat and allow it to cool for about 30–45 minutes. The grease will rise to the top. Take folded paper towel and gently set it on top of the gravy, allowing the towel to absorb only the grease. Gently throw the paper towel into the trash. Repeat until all the grease has been removed.

Sore Throat Remedy—Grandma McKneely taught me this one many years ago. In a glass, combine 1 tablespoon salt, 2 tablespoons white vinegar, and 2 aspirins. Using a spoon, crush the aspirins and dissolve the salt. Add 4–6 ounces of hot water. Stir. Check the temperature of the mixture. If it's not warm enough, pop it into the microwave for a few seconds until warm. (Baby, don't be stupid and scald your throat with boiling water.) Gargle with the mixture. Repeat the process every hour until no longer needed. Two times usually does the trick. This is one nasty-tasting concoction, but it will knock out a sore throat.

Tabasco Sauce—There are very few dishes that can't be made better with a splash or two of Tabasco sauce. It's not as hot as you think. Take a chance. Live a little!

Tony Chachere's Original Creole Seasoning—I've run out of this twice in my life. Both times, the kitchen was closed until I received my shipment. (I order it by the case.) If you can't find it locally, order it online or through the 800 number. You'll be glad you did!

White Rice—Because I could never seem to get the hang of steaming rice in the right amount of water, Mama taught me to boil it. In a large stockpot, boil six to eight cups of water with a pinch of salt and a tablespoon of margarine. Add two cups of rice and cook until done. (Tasting to see if it still crunches.) Once done, pour into a colander and run under cold water. Perfect fluffy rice every time. For even fancier rice, add a tablespoon of dried parsley to the water.

Where to Get the Good Stuff

Knorr Concentrated Chicken Flavor Broth
Bestfoods Specialty Products
Indianapolis, IN 46221
(800) 338-8831

Louisiana Fish Fry Products, Ltd.
5267 Plank Road
Baton Rouge, LA 70805
(800) 356-2905
www.louisianafishfry.com

Oak Grove Smokehouse, Inc.
Jambalaya Mix
17618 Old Jefferson Hwy.
Prairieville, LA 70769
(225) 673-6857

Tabasco Sauce
McIlhenny Company
Avery Island, LA 70513
(800) 634-9599
www.tabasco.com

Tony Chachere's Original Seasoning
P.O. Box 1639
Opelousas, LA 70571
(800) 551-9066
www.tonychachere.com

Velveeta Cheese
www.velveeta.com
(800) 634-1984

Zatarain's Gumbo Filé
Zatarain's Seasoned Fish Fry
New Orleans, LA 70114
www.zatarain.com

Where Is That Recipe?

Final Thoughts

Through the years and through the tears, the heartaches and the abuse, I wouldn't change a thing. It is through the suffering that I have become the Man that I am today. I am looking forward to the rest of this incredible journey that we call life. I am ready for whatever may come my way, because in my heart I have: faith, hope and love.

When this journey is over, and I have made it to the other side, reunited with all those that have gone before me, know that I too will be there...looking after you.

"Love yourself first."

Give the Gift of

Lessons Learned While Cooking...

FROM THE HEART

to Your Friends and Colleagues

CHECK YOUR LEADING BOOKSTORE OR ORDER HERE

❑ **YES**, I want _____ copies of *Lessons Learned While Cooking ... From the Heart* at $19.95 each, plus $4.95 shipping per book (California residents please add $1.70 sales tax per book). Canadian orders must be accompanied by a postal money order in U.S. funds. Allow 15 days for delivery.

My check or money order for $_____ is enclosed.

Please charge my: ❑ Visa ❑ MasterCard

❑ Discover ❑ American Express

Name _____

Organization _____

Address _____

City/State/Zip _____

Phone_____ E-mail _____

Card # _____

Exp. Date_____ Signature _____

Please make your check payable and return to:

Always Productions

P.O. Box 33836 • San Diego, CA 92163-3836

Call your credit card order to: 619-296-5747